The LionheART Guide to Editing Fiction

Fiction

UK Edition

I0162158

by

Karen Perkins

LionheART Publishing House

LionheART Publishing House
Harrogate
UK

www.lionheartgalleries.co.uk
www.facebook.com/lionheartpublishing
publishing@lionheartgalleries.co.uk

First published in Great Britain in 2014 by
LionheART Publishing House
Copyright © Karen Perkins 2014
ISBN: 978-1-910115-06-0

Classification: Editing, Formatting, Indie, Self-Publishing,
Writing, Publishing, Guides, Self-Help

Cover Design by CC Morgan Creative Visuals

Contents

Introduction

Welcome to *The LionheART Guide To Editing Fiction*. As the proprietor of LionheART Publishing House, I have helped over a hundred books come to publication in the past year alone, and whilst there are numerous comprehensive grammar guides out there, it is not always that easy to pick out the elements that are most useful to us as authors of fiction.

A reader should not be able to tell whether a book has been published independently or traditionally just by reading it – and quite simply, they also deserve a self-published book to be of the same high standard as a book from one of the major publishing houses. This means getting all the elements right – not just the story, but also the editing, formatting and cover.

This simple and user-friendly guide is for authors who want to be intimately involved – and in control – of every aspect of their book, and is full of tips to help you decipher the punctuation and grammatical rules and apply them to your own work. The areas I have highlighted are the ones I come across most often when editing and I also detail the method I use when editing and polishing a manuscript for publication.

However comprehensively you edit your own work, there is no substitute for fresh, objective eyes and I do recommend you hire an independent editor once you have completed your self-editing process. Most editors charge by the hour, so the higher the standard of your manuscript before you submit it, the higher the standard of your manuscript after editing – and the lower the final cost – so it is worth polishing your manuscript yourself as much as possible first.

*

As writers we are wordsmiths, creating a world, characters and story with language, and punctuation is one of the tools of language. To ignore it, except for rare exceptions, to me is like Monet painting with badly mixed colours, or Michelangelo attempting to sculpt using a hammer when a chisel is needed.

Words are what we do, language is our medium and punctuation is our tool. When I write, I want to take my readers to my world, to join my characters on their journey, to experience their challenges, traumas and desires. I want them to take this journey with me, without noticing the individual words, full stops or commas. I want them to lose themselves in the story, not in the mechanics of it, and this will only happen if all the elements are right.

*

I have used four main sources in compiling this guide (and a full bibliography is included at the end): *The Chicago Manual of Style 16th Edition; New Hart's Rules; New Oxford Dictionary For Writers and Editors* and *The Creative Writing Coursebook.*

Karen Perkins
LionheART Publishing House
www.lionheartgalleries.co.uk

The LionheART Guide To Editing Fiction

UK Edition

Before You Edit

1. Preparing To Edit

The first – and probably the hardest – thing to do when you've finished your manuscript is to put it aside and leave it alone for a month or two. Don't pick it up during this time. Don't make any changes. If something occurs to you, make a note in a notebook, but do not open that file until it's time to edit.

When editing your own work, the biggest challenge is to be objective; something that is virtually impossible when you have spent months or years working on your book, living in your characters' world and putting your soul and emotions into their story. On top of that, when the story is still fresh in your mind it is far too easy to miss very simple mistakes – you know what you meant to write when you wrote the words, and that is often what you read rather than the actual words used.

When you are ready to start the editing process, first of all read it through as you would any other novel. Don't make any corrections or notes, just read. Then it's time to get the red pen out, whether biro or computerized. The new versions of Word have a very useful review function where you can track all your changes so you can go through the manuscript, then go through the changes and make sure you agree (even your edits need editing).

2. Tracking Changes

To enable this function in Word, click on the *Review* tab at the top of the screen, which will give you a number of options (see screenshot below). In the middle of the toolbar is the option to *Track Changes*. Click on this, then click on the dropdown box showing *Final: Show Markup* and select *Simple Markup* or *Final* depending on which version of Word you are using. This is to stop you being distracted by the changes (which will all be marked in colour) and also allows you to better assess the punctuation.

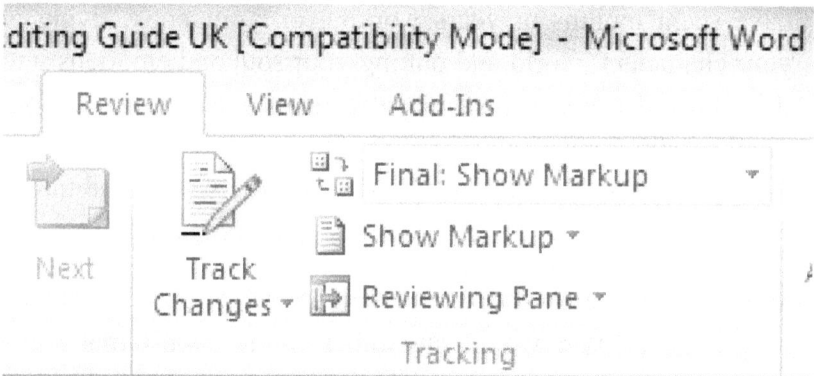

diting Guide UK [Compatibility Mode] - Microsoft Word

Review   View   Add-Ins

Next   Track Changes ▾   Final: Show Markup ▾

Show Markup ▾

Reviewing Pane ▾

Tracking

3. Formatting Marks

The next step is to show the formatting marks – line breaks, tabs, paragraph breaks etc. By editing these at this stage, it makes the final formatting much easier, as well as speeding up the process.

To enable this function, click on the *Home* tab on the toolbar, then click on the *Show/Hide* button (the paragraph break symbol shown below), again positioned in the centre of the toolbar.

tibility Mo

Add-Ins

¶

This will show every formatting mark in your manuscript, including spaces between the words. As indie publishers, our largest market is usually e-books, in particular Kindle, and it's good practice to prepare your manuscript with the end result in mind. This means using paragraph breaks rather than line breaks, making sure there are no extra paragraph breaks (which may result in blank pages in the final e-book), no extra spaces, no tabs etc.

Line break symbol:

Paragraph break symbol:

Tab symbol:

Space symbol:

4. Indents

Next we come to indents. Many authors use the tab button or a number of spaces, but this will result in a badly formatted e-book. Instead, assign your full manuscript to the *Normal* style – although this may have happened automatically depending on which version of Word you are using.

The style tools are under the *Home* tab, on the right-hand half of the toolbar in Word 2010:

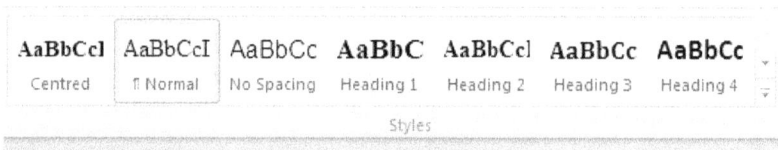

AaBbCcI	AaBbCcI	AaBbCc	**AaBbC**	AaBbCcI	AaBbCc	**AaBbCc**
Centred	¶ Normal	No Spacing	Heading 1	Heading 2	Heading 3	Heading 4

Styles

As you can see, if a style is assigned to your text, its box will be highlighted in yellow. If nothing is highlighted, select the whole of your document (by pressing *ctrl* and *a*), then right click on the *Normal* style box, which will give you the following options:

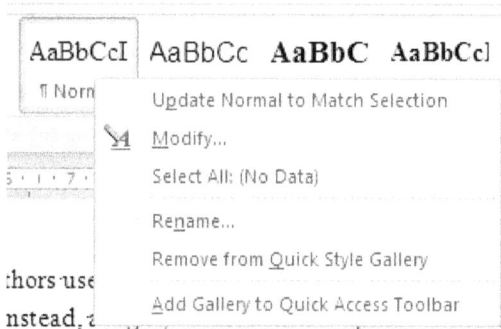

AaBbCcI	AaBbCc	**AaBbC**	AaBbCcI

¶ Norm

Update Normal to Match Selection

Modify...

Select All: (No Data)

Rename...

Remove from Quick Style Gallery

Add Gallery to Quick Access Toolbar

Right click on *Modify*, which brings up the following box:

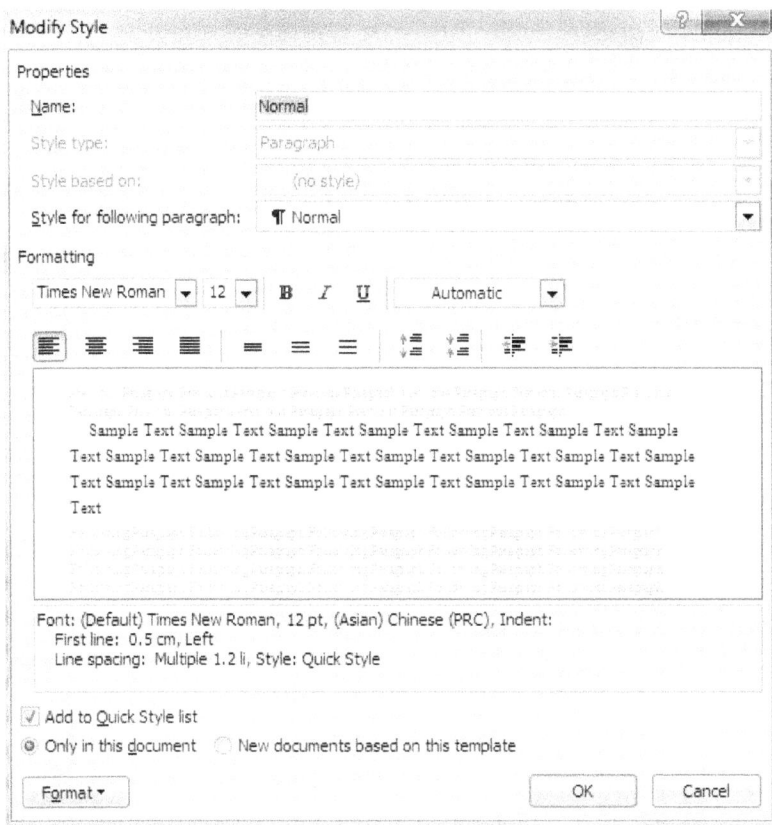

Here you will set the parameters for laying out your manuscript, which is very useful to prepare the common formatting elements between the Kindle, EPUB (usually Smashwords) and paperback formats – again saving you time and lessening the potential for formatting errors in your final files.

Always set the font to Times New Roman – this is the only font the e-readers can all handle (although you are free to use whichever font you wish for your paperbacks as long as you hold the proper license) – and set the size to 11 or 12 depending on your style of book and personal preference. Then ensure the bold, italics and underlining buttons are not enabled.

Click on *Format* at the left-hand bottom corner and you will have a list of options:

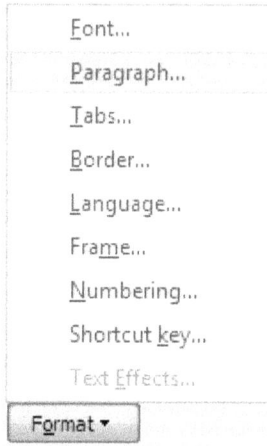

Click on *Paragraph* to bring up the next dialogue box and complete it as follows:

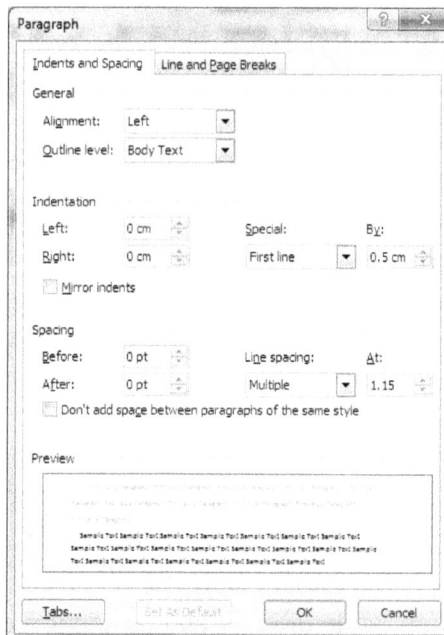

Alignment: Left
Outline Levels: Body Text
Indentation:
Left: 0 cm
Right: 0 cm
Special: First Line 0.5 cm
Spacing:
Before: 0 pt
After: 0 pt
Line Spacing: Multiple 1.15

Then click *OK*, which takes you back to the previous dialogue box. Click *OK* here as well to go back to your manuscript.

If you are preparing your manuscript for submission to agents rather than self-publishing, read their submission requirements carefully and enter the appropriate values in the dialogue boxes above.

5. Chapter Headings

The next stage is to format your chapter headings, which will make it easier for you to navigate your manuscript as well as check that your chapters are numbered correctly and consistently. An added bonus is that you will be able to easily insert a table of contents when you come to format your book.

Scroll through your manuscript and insert a page break (*ctrl* and *enter*) at the end of each chapter as well as after every section of your front and end papers (title page, copyright page, acknowledgements, dedication, author page etc.).

Select your first heading (whether an item in your front papers, prologue or first chapter) and assign the *Heading 1* style by selecting the heading and right clicking on *Heading 1*:

AaBbCcI	AaBbCcI	AaBbCcI	**AaBbC**	AaBbCcI	AaBbCc	**AaBbCc**
Centred	¶ Normal	No Spacing	Heading 1	Heading 2	Heading 3	Heading 4

Styles

Now to modify *Heading 1* by right-clicking on it as we did before with *Normal*:

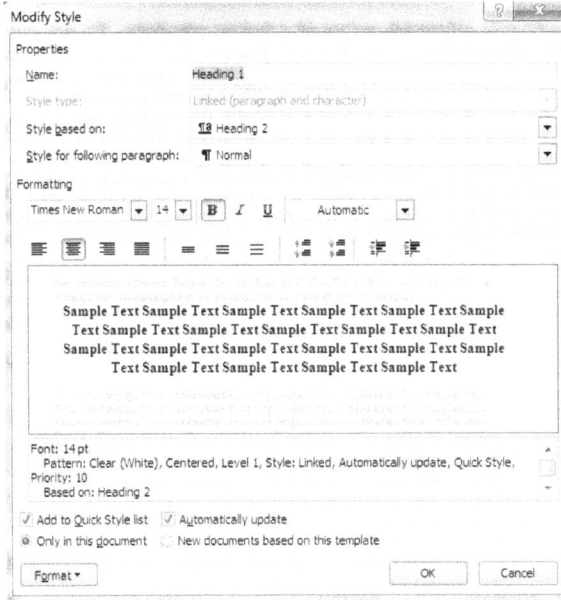

Keep the font as Times New Roman, but here use a larger size. My standard is 14 as this looks best on e-readers. By ticking the *Automatically Update* box near the bottom, if you want to change your heading style later, you can do so on one heading in the manuscript and it will carry through to all your other headings (although it is always worth double-checking that this has worked). Next click on *Format* then *Paragraph* as before to bring up the second dialogue box:

This shows the LionheART standard settings as follows:

Alignment: Centered
Outline Levels: Level 1
Indentation:
Left: 0 cm
Right: 0 cm
Special: None
Spacing:
Before: 0 pt
After: 0 pt
Line Spacing: Multiple 1.15

Click *OK* to close the box and again in the next one.

Select each heading in turn and apply it to *Heading 1* by clicking on the box. If your navigation pane is open on the left-hand side of your screen, click on the left-hand icon and you will see a list of your headings appear.

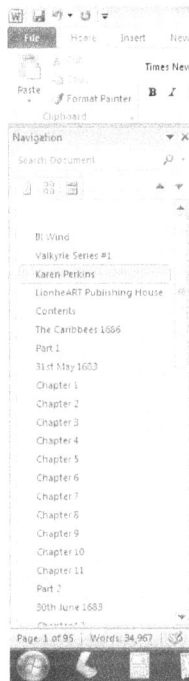

If the navigation pane is not visible, click on *Find* in the top right-hand corner of the toolbar under the *Home* tab, which should bring it up.

You are now ready to start editing.

The Editing Process

There are four main principles to editing:

1. Check, Check and Check Again

2. Make Detailed Notes

3. Be Consistent

4. Be Tough

1. Check, Check And Check Again

After I have done my initial read through, I then go through the manuscript at least four times.

The first edit is the most comprehensive and intensive. Not only do I check all spellings, grammar and punctuation, but also every date and every name such as real-life characters and brand names etc. Basically everything that can be verified in Google, no matter how sure I am that it's right. Sometimes it isn't.

Then leave the manuscript a day to refresh your brain before reading it through again. This gives you the opportunity not only to edit your edits, but your subconscious will have been working during this day off, and things you didn't pick out on your first pass will jump out at you on the second – especially if you read it aloud.

Then take a week off before reading again. At this point I click on the *Show/Hide* icon to hide the formatting marks – this will make it easier to see if any full stops or closing quotation marks are missing.

Again take a day off, then either print the book out or transfer it to your e-reader. If you have a Kindle, you could also email it – the email address can be found under *Manage Your Kindle* on Amazon in your *Account* section, but don't forget to authorize your Kindle to accept emails from your normal email address (this can be found in the same section). By reading on paper or an e-reader rather than a computer screen, it gives you a more genuine reading experience and you will spot more errors. Also, to avoid interrupting the flow of your read, just highlight the areas which need attention with maybe a short note rather than making the edits straight away. Then go through your highlights and notes and carefully transfer them to the master file, bearing in mind that it is very easy to add mistakes at this stage, which would undo all the hard work you've already done.

If there are a lot of edits to make, it is worth leaving it a day or two then going over it again until you're confident of the final result.

Next do a spell and grammar check using Word's spellchecker: a final check to ensure nothing has slipped through and you haven't left out a space, for example, between two words.

Before publishing, it is also a very good idea to have two or three friends or fellow authors to beta read for you. Two pairs of eyes (or more) are always better than one, and they may pick up on something you've missed. It is important, however, that you choose people you trust, not only to know what they're doing, but also to be brutally honest with you. It is never nice to receive your manuscript back full of crossings out and/or suggestions, but it is far better to address these things now rather than after you have published your book and any issues are highlighted in public reviews.

Then edit again. Sorry!

A trap many self-published authors fall into, especially with our first books, is to publish too soon. The only way to avoid this is to take your time to make sure your book is as good as it can be. Having said that, and whilst it is important to spend as much time as required on the editing, it is equally important to know when you've finished. If you are reversing changes you have made, then it is probably time to stop.

2. Make Detailed Notes

There is nothing more frustrating to a reader than a character changing name or hair colour halfway through the story, or injuries disappearing, or there being two Tuesdays in a week etc. The only way to keep track of all these details is to write them down and keep checking as you edit. Even if you made notes when writing your book, start again so that you are only recording information that is in your final draft. I divide my own notes into four main categories and refer to them constantly throughout the editing process:

Characters – including any and all details given about them and injuries they suffer throughout the book, even down to the colour and make of their car.

Places – spelling, location, distance and travelling time between etc.

Chronology – all dates, ages and passages of time.

Style – for example, *okay*, *ok* and *OK* are all correct, but only if the same form is used throughout. Similarly with *t-shirt* or *tee-shirt*.

3. Be Consistent

The better your notes are (and the more you refer to them), the more consistent your novel will be. Any inconsistencies may jolt your reader out of the story and have them looking back to check details, spoiling their reading experience and enjoyment of your book. It may also discourage them from buying your next one; so again, it is well worth taking the time to ensure there are no errors of this type.

4. Be Tough

There is no point in an editor being kind, whether editing your own work or someone else's. If you are not tough on yourself your readers, especially reviewers, will be – and in public. Yes, write your first draft for yourself, enjoy it and be kind to yourself at that stage. Then edit your work with readers and reviewers in mind. Be as picky as you can, be harsh, and make your book the best it can be. Look hard for errors and question everything. No, it is not a pleasant process, but you will do justice to your characters and story.

And don't forget to give yourself a pat on the back when you have finished, don't destroy your self-confidence. No writer's early drafts are perfect – they're not supposed to be, they're early drafts! That is what the editing process is for: to find and eliminate errors and inconsistencies, and to polish your story until it gleams – and it *will* shine. Believe in yourself, not only as a writer, but also as an editor.

Common Editing Issues

As I mentioned in my introduction, there are many comprehensive guides to grammar and punctuation available, and this section focuses on what I have found to be the most common errors in four areas:

1. Spelling

2. Grammar

3. Punctuation

4. Gremlins

1. Spelling

This section includes a number of words that are commonly misspelt or handled incorrectly; for example, the words *on to* are frequently put together as *onto*. Whilst this is often correct in US English, it isn't in UK English, yet it isn't natural for many British writers to use *on to*.

I have divided this section up into seven main parts to make reference easier, and have explained the rules with examples:

1. Capital Letters

2. Hyphens

3. Italics

4. -ise Versus -ize

5. Common Misspellings

1. Capital Letters

When should a word be capitalized? When should it start with the lower case? Why is the same word capitalized in one sentence yet not in another?

There is a trend in the publishing industry to use fewer capitals now than in previous years, and I'll start with the areas that are always capitalized:

1. The beginning of a sentence.
2. Somebody's name or a place name.
3. Each word in the title of a book, film, song etc. It is also acceptable, although becoming less common, to capitalize only the important words in a title, leaving words such as *the*, *a*, *on*, *in*, etc. in lower case. Whichever method you choose, however, it is important to be consistent.
4. Chapter headings and subheadings (as above).

But when is the rule not so hard and fast?

i) Proper Nouns Versus Common Nouns:

Proper nouns (specific names *of* something) are capitalized; common nouns (general names *for* something) are not.

Nouns denoting relationships, such as Mum and Dad; titles of office such as Prime Minister; and ranks, such as General, Officer, can be either a proper noun or a common noun depending on the way they are used in the sentence:
'*Hi, Mum.*' versus '*This is my mum.*'
'*Prime Minister, David Cameron.*' versus '*David Cameron, the prime minister.*'
'*The brigadier sat down.*' versus '*Please sit down, Brigadier.*'

God, Allah and the names of other deities are also capitalized when used as names, referring to *the* deity, but not when referring to *a* deity. So:

'Praise to Allah!'

'For God's sake!'

'A tribute to the gods.'

ii) Abbreviations And Acronyms

These are usually capitalized, but there are notable exceptions:

i) *a.m.* and *p.m.*

ii) *etc.*

iii) *e.g.* and *i.e.*

iv) most units of measure (e.g. *cm*, *kg* etc.)

v) many scholarly abbreviations (e.g. *ibid.*, *sic* etc. Although *MS* for manuscript)

iii) Compass Points

Compass points themselves are lowercase (*heading north, a west wind, north-westerly*) unless they describe a region of the world/country or cultural entity (*the North, Northern Ireland, the mysterious East*). Also *North Africa* denotes a specific region and is capitalized; *northern Africa* denotes a general area and is not.

iv) Organizations And Brand Names

When used as a noun, these are always capitalized (e.g. *Hoover*, *Google*), but when used as a verb, they are lowercase (e.g. *I googled him*, *You hoovered yesterday*).

v) Trends Moving Away From Using Capitals:

Emphasis

Capital letters have historically been used for emphasis, but nowadays, italics are more usually used, e.g. 'You think I'm Jealous?' becomes 'You think I'm *jealous*?'

2. Hyphens

I cover eight main areas in this section:

i) Compound Terms
ii) Capitalizing Hyphenated Compounds In Titles
iii) Ages
iv) Numbers
v) Colours
vi) Fractions
vii) Compass Points
viii) Noun Versus Verb

i) Compound Terms

Compound terms can be spelled either as two words, hyphenated or single words, and there is a move in the publishing industry towards less hyphenation. The best way to ensure you spell a compound term correctly is by using a good dictionary such as *The Oxford Dictionary*, and refer to it often.

A compound modifier (whether adjective or participle) *before* the noun is hyphenated and open when it comes *after* the noun:
She's a well-known woman versus *She is well known*
He's a good-looking man versus *He is good looking*

Compound terms using an adverb are not hyphenated, e.g. smartly dressed, fairly handled.

ii) Capitalizing Hyphenated Compounds In Titles

Always capitalize the first element and only capitalize the second if it is a noun or proper adjective, or if it is equally as important as the first element:
Eighteenth-Century Poetry, Tool-Maker, Non-Christian

Do not capitalize the second element if it modifies the first element or both elements together make a single word:
French-speaking People, Large-sized Library, B-flat Minor, Re-establish, Self-sustaining

iii) Ages:

A *three-year-old (child)* is hyphenated whether used as a noun or adjective.

Seven years old, seventeen years of age is always open as the number modifies the noun *years* rather than the individual referred to.

iv) Numbers:

Historically, when the number is used on its own, e.g. *there are fifty-two cards in a pack*, it was hyphenated if between one and a hundred, but there is a move within the publishing industry to reduce hyphens, and it is becoming more common to leave this open: *fifty two cards in a pack*.

An advantage of omitting the hyphen is that it prevents confusion with numbers used as modifiers, which *are* always hyphenated, e.g. *the fifty-second floor, a hundred-metre race*.

v) Colours:

Colours are hyphenated when they appear before the noun, but not after a noun, e.g. *light-blue dress, reddish-brown stain, black-and-white mini-skirt, blue-green algae.* But: *the clouds are snow white, the horse is brown and white, the sea is blue green, the sauce is reddish brown.* By using a hyphen in, say, *light-blue dress*, it makes it clear to the reader that the modifier *light* refers to the colour blue and not to the dress itself.

vi) Fractions

Simple fractions are hyphenated when used as nouns and open when adjectives, e.g. *three-quarters of the cake* versus *a three quarter moon.*

Conversely, compound fractions are open when used as nouns and hyphenated when adjectives, e.g. *a half mile* versus *a half-mile run.*

vii) Compass Points

These are hyphenated in UK English (*north-east*) unless they are capitalized (*South East Asia*) but are a single word in US English (*northeast*; *Southeast Asia*)

viii) Noun Versus Verb

Nouns which are open when used as a noun, e.g. *machine gun* are nevertheless hyphenated when used as a verb, e.g. *machine-gunned* or *machine-gunning.*

3. Italics

<u>Use Italics for:</u>

1. Thoughts and internal dialogue
2. Stressing words (although use sparingly)
3. Titles in text
4. Names of ships, aircraft etc.
5. Stage directions in plays

If you want to stress a word in an italicized phrase or passage, put it into normal (Roman type), e.g. *"You think I'm* jealous*?"*

<u>A Note on Foreign Words.</u>

Historically, isolated words or phrases in a foreign language were italicized, but the publishing industry is now moving away from this and leaving them in normal (Roman) type.

4. -ise Versus -ize

It is understandable to assume that UK English always uses *-ise*, while US English is always *-ize*, as *-ise* has traditionally been more common in the UK, but the UK publishing industry is moving towards *-ize* and it is now acceptable to use either for most words (as long as you are consistent throughout your book), although some are always *-ise*, such as:

advertise, advise, apprise, arise, chastise, circumcise, comprise, compromise, demise, despise, devise, disenfranchise, disguise, enterprise, excise, exercise, improvise, incise, merchandise, premise, revise, supervise, surmise, surprise, televise.

A quick note on practise: this is only *-ise* when used as a verb (and never *-ize*). When used as a noun, the spelling is practice.

5. Common Misspellings

Many of us are in the habit of using the incorrect forms of some very common words in our writing – probably because they are correct in the US and have become common here – just not in the publishing industry:

1. all right not alright
2. any more not anymore
3. focused not focussed
4. for ever not forever (unless forever young)
5. no one not no-one
6. on to not onto
7. till not 'til
8. blond versus blonde – blond when referring to a man, blonde for a woman

The easiest way to deal with them when editing is to use the *Find and Replace* function in Word (top right hand of the *Home* toolbar). But take care, especially when searching for *onto* to make sure you include a space both before and after in the *Find* and *Replace* boxes to ensure you don't inadvertently add a space in the middle of longer words which contain the sequence *onto*. You don't want to turn *pronto* into *pron to*, *promontory* to *promon tory* or *contort* into *con tort*.

If you are still unsure about the spelling of a word, whether it should have a hyphen, or be two words etc. two excellent resources are:

www.oxforddictionaries.com
You can search under *British and World English* or *US English* as appropriate.

New Oxford Dictionary for Writers and Editors
This is the most useful dictionary I have on my shelf and includes many entries you wouldn't find in a more traditional dictionary. It contains many words which are commonly misspelt, and shows the difference in spelling depending on whether the word is used as a noun or verb, or whether it should be hyphenated or capitalized etc. It also often explains which spelling is British and which American, and includes foreign and specialist terms as well as references to historical figures and literature. This resource is now available in the Oxford online dictionary for subscribers.

2. Grammar

In this section I have concentrated on six main areas where I see authors having the most difficulty or questions:

1. Tense

2. Dialogue Tags

3. Contractions

4. Numbers

5. Adverbs

6. Participles

7. Sentence Construction And Word Order

1. Tense

There are two main tenses used in fiction today: past simple and present. Whichever tense you choose to write in, it needs to be consistent; otherwise it is confusing for the reader and interrupts the flow of your narrative. It's also important to avoid the passive tense wherever possible.

i) Writing In The Past Tense

This is by far the most common tense used, and generally the one we as writers are most comfortable with. The past simple is the most basic past tense and used to describe actions or events that have already happened.

The main issue I come across here is when events (often backstory or flashbacks) are presented. To carry on in the past simple puts them at the same point of time as the rest of the plot, but by definition they happened previously and so need to be written in the past perfect. This communicates to the reader that we are looking back from one point in the past to a point further in the past. Many authors struggle with this, and some actively avoid it as it can necessitate the use of *had had*. Whilst I agree it is best to avoid this wherever possible by constructing the sentence differently, this is not always possible without causing other problems and it is better to include *had had* rather than cause confusion by using the wrong tense.

Consider the following passage:

He marched to the door and shouted for Klara. I flinched. When did he think Klara had had chance to introduce me to anyone? Why had he not made any introductions himself? He had not even introduced his son – I had been forced to guess that was who he was.

The book is written in the past simple (*He marched to the door and shouted for Klara. I flinched*) then looks further back (*When did he think Klara had had chance to introduce me to anyone? Why had he not made any introductions himself?*).

By missing the past perfect or refusing to use two *hads*, the passage would read:

He marched to the door and shouted for Klara. I flinched. When did he think Klara had chance to introduce me to anyone? Why did he not make any introductions himself? He did not even introduce his son – I was forced to guess that's who he was.

The two characters (Gabriella and Jan) are alone. It is clear that Klara is not present from the first sentence, and Jan's son Erik left the room a few sentences previously, but writing in the simple past would imply that Klara and Erik are with Gabriella and Jan, and introductions can be made at the time.

Dialogue is written in the present tense, including your characters' thoughts, unless the characters are looking back and referring to something that happened in their past.

ii) Writing In The Present Tense

This is becoming more popular in today's fiction market, but rarely comes naturally to an author. If you choose to write in the present tense, be very careful to be consistent, and only dip into the past tense when writing flashbacks or as appropriate in dialogue. When you are editing, it is even more important to do at least one of your reads aloud to help you spot any slips into the past.

iii) The Passive Tense

The Oxford Dictionary defines a passive verb as "having a subject which is undergoing the action of the verb, rather than carrying it out", e.g. *The apple was eaten* as opposed to *He ate the apple* or *The door swung open* as opposed to *My husband opened the door.*

The first example raises a question in the mind of the reader – *who* ate the apple? The second is factually incorrect – doors rarely swing open by themselves (unless of course you're writing a ghost story) but need someone to exert a force on them.

As this second example shows, there are occasions when the passive tense works; but even here, if your manuscript is riddled with the passive tense, it diminishes the impact of the occasional correct use.

Usually, the passive tense does not work well in fiction, it diminishes the impact of your sentence and the reader has to wait until the end of the sentence, or even a future sentence to find out who is doing the action, which can be annoying. It's therefore best avoided unless there is a valid reason for using it.

<u>iv) Subjunctive</u>

Paraphrasing from *The Oxford Dictionary*, the subjunctive is a special form of a verb which expresses a wish or possibility instead of a fact.

E.g. *The CPS recommend that he face trial* is correct as facing trial is a wish of the CPS (Crown Prosecution Service), as opposed to the certainty of *He faces trial.*

She felt as though she were in a daze is correct as it is only a possibility; as opposed to the certainty of *She was in a daze.*

2. Dialogue Tags

It is usual when writing dialogue to stick mainly to the dialogue tags *I said*, *he said*, *she said*. This way the reader doesn't notice them and the dialogue flows more naturally.

Of course, there are some exceptions, e.g. *he asked, she replied.*

If you use a wide variety of dialogue tags, such as *she wondered, he answered, they chorused* etc. this can be distracting for your reader. Do you want your reader to think about the wondrous variety of dialogue tags you've come up with or to be lost in your story and your characters' world?

3. Contractions

It is now standard to use contractions (*isn't, hasn't, don't, let's* etc.) in novels as this creates a more natural reading experience. However, if you are writing a historical novel, you can hint at historical language by avoiding the use of contractions in your narrative (although dialogue is different – the use of contractions helps to make the dialogue flow better and seem naturalistic).

4. Numbers

Numbers should be spelled out in words wherever possible, although there are exceptions:

1. Large numbers of three or more digits, unless round hundreds or thousands
2. Percentages (*90 per cent*)
3. Weights and measures (see below)
4. Exact amounts of money
5. Sets or lists of numbers
6. Inclusive pairs of numbers such as years, pages, house numbers etc. (i.e. *1–10*)
7. *1990s* or *the nineties* – no apostrophe

Regardless of the above, numbers starting a sentence should always be spelled out in words, although this does not always work, for example in the case of years or very large, complicated numbers. It is better in this case to reconstruct the sentence so that it does not begin with the number.

Weights And Measures

If you are using the abbreviated form of the unit of weight or measurement, then use digits; if you are using the full name of the unit of weight or measurement, then spell the number out, e.g. *100 kg* or *one hundred kilogrammes*.

For heights, there is no space between the feet and inches, e.g. 6'1".

5. Adverbs

Adverbs are defined by *The Oxford Dictionary* as "a word or phrase that modifies the meaning of an adjective, verb, or other adverb, expressing manner, place, time, or degree" and usually end in -ly, e.g. *fully, speedily.*

Use them sparingly, only if absolutely(!) necessary, and never at the end of a sentence if it can be avoided.

6. Participles

Participles are defined by *The Chicago Manual of Style* as "a nonfinite verb that is not limited by person, number or mood, but does have tense." Take care to use past and present participles correctly. Past participles end in *-ed* and indicate that the verb's action has been completed; present participles end in *-ing* and indicate that the verb's action is ongoing.

Take care to avoid dangling participles—a participle that doesn't refer to the nearest subject. They make the sentence difficult to read or make sense of, e.g. *"Being an excellent teacher, Mr. Smith gets good results."* By beginning the sentence with *being an excellent teacher*, this reads as if it is the speaker who is an excellent teacher, rather than Mr. Smith. Compare the above sentence to: *"Mr. Smith is an excellent teacher and gets good results."*

Present participles can be a useful way of avoiding using *that* in a sentence and helping the flow of your narrative, e.g. *Chickens that scattered at my feet* versus *Chickens scattering at my feet.*

Participial adjectives can also be extremely useful as long as they are not overdone, e.g. *walking stick* or *dwindling pile*.

7. Sentence Construction And Word Order

If there are two subjects in the sentence, is it clear which is causing the action? Consider the difference between the two following sentences:

The shadow was long and thin with a number of branches that stretched away from me and *Stretching away from me, the shadow was long and thin with a number of branches.*

The first sentence reads as though the branches are stretching away from the narrator, and the second makes it clear the shadow stretches away from the narrator.

Also, try to avoid ending a sentence with an adverb (such as *easily, simply, really*) or preposition such as *with*, e.g. *the woman Michael had fallen in love with* versus *the woman who had stolen Michael's heart.*

3. Punctuation

Again, I have concentrated on the main areas which give difficulty:

1. Commas

2. Semicolons

3. Colons

4. Exclamation And Question Marks

5. Dialogue

6. Possessive Apostrophes

7. En dashes And Em dashes

8. Ellipses

1. Commas

The comma is the most common form of punctuation – and the most often incorrectly used. A misplaced or missing comma can change the whole meaning of a sentence and it is important to understand their use. When editing, this is another area where reading aloud – whether to yourself or another person – can be very useful.

i) Separating Adjectives

Whether a comma is used between adjectives depends on the type of adjective used: qualitative or classifying.

Qualitative (or gradable) adjectives, such as *happy*, *fat*, *small* and *dark* are separated by commas. Qualitative adjectives can be identified by assessing whether they work with modifiers such as *very* or can have -*er* added to them (*happier, fatter, smaller*). Also, if the adjectives are hyphenated, such as *well-known* or *good-looking*, they are also separated by a comma.

Classifying adjectives, such as *black English edible* etc. are not separated by commas.

Another way to distinguish between the two types is by considering whether they could be separated by *and*, e.g. *A happy, fat man . . .* could be expressed *A happy and fat man . . .* and are qualitative. If *and* doesn't work, for example in the phrase *English medieval poetry*, the adjectives are classifying.

If you have adjectives of both types together, they are not separated by a comma.

ii) The Serial Or Oxford Comma

Whether a comma should be used before *and* in a list of three or more items is debatable, and this is very much a case of your personal preference. At LionheART Publishing House, I do not include a comma before *and* if the list is comprised of single words, and do use the comma if it is a list of phrases. Therefore, a list of colours would read: *red, orange, yellow, green, blue, indigo and violet*; whereas a list of coloured clothing would read: *a smart red jacket, a tatty orange blouse, yellow threadbare trousers, and high-heeled green shoes* (although I wouldn't suggest you try wearing this combination!).

Whichever system you choose to use, the most important thing – once again – is to be consistent.

iii) Relative Clauses

There are two types of relative clause: defining and non-defining (also called restrictive and non-restrictive). A defining clause can't be left out without affecting the sentence's meaning and is not enclosed by commas, e.g. *The people who live there are rich.* Leaving out *who live there* would change the meaning to *all the people are rich*, and so there are no commas.

A non-defining clause adds detail to the sentence and does not affect the meaning if it is omitted, e.g. *This is a big house, which makes it a target, and the thought of you being on your own concerns me.* Leaving out *which makes it a target* doesn't affect the meaning but adds information and emphasis.

iv) Parenthetical Clauses

These usually use commas, although can also be marked off with brackets or en dashes, and need a comma at the end as well as beginning, e.g. *I finished my ale as John walked in, stamping mud from his boots, and Mary jumped up.*

v) Introductory Clauses Or Adverbs

Historically, commas were used when a sentence is introduced by an introductory clause, e.g. *When you're ready, we'll be off* or by most adverbs (a modifying word usually ending in *-ly*), e.g. *Hurriedly, they walked to the car* (although this sentence could be better reworked to avoid the adverb completely: *They were in a hurry as they walked to the car*).

However, the comma is not needed if the introductory clause is short, and the publishing industry now tends to leave them out wherever possible – but take care that the meaning of your sentence is unaltered by the omission.

As shown in the last sentence, if an adverb such as *however, moreover, therefore* or *already* begins a sentence, it *is* followed by a comma. These adverbs are also fully contained by commas when used in the middle of a sentence. An exception to the rule is when *however* is used as a modifier, e.g. *However hard I try it won't work.*

2. Semicolons

A semicolon is a stronger separation than a comma and there are three main uses:

1. Between two independent clauses which are not joined by a conjunction (e.g. *and*, *but*).
2. In a complex series or list – especially if the items in the list themselves contain commas.
3. To divide two or more main clauses which are closely related, complement each other, and could stand as two sentences on their own.

A clause following a semicolon *adds* to the previous clause.

3. Colons

A colon points forward in a variety of ways:

1. From a cause to an effect.
2. From a general statement to an example.
3. From a premise to a conclusion.
4. When introducing a list.
5. When introducing an element or series of elements, and does the work of the phrase *as follows*.
6. When doing the work of linking words such as *namely*, *that is*, *as*, *for example*, *for instance*, *because*, *therefore*.

In UK English, colons are always followed by the lower case (except proper nouns etc.), but in US English, a capital letter follows a colon if the sentence is grammatically complete.

A clause following a colon *explains* the previous clause.

4. Exclamation and Question Marks

Two rules here – use them sparingly and only use one at a time.

A book littered with exclamation marks can annoy the reader and has the effect of reducing the impact of sentences you are trying to emphasize. Only use one if you really need one.

Only use question marks when the sentence is in fact a question. *I wonder if he's on his way* isn't actually a question, even if somebody answers.

The use of !! or ?! etc. shouts, 'Self-published book!' to a reader, so choose which one is most appropriate and delete the extra.

5. Dialogue

i) Quotation Marks

The UK standard is to use single quotation marks around all speech, and double quotation marks for quotes within the dialogue, whilst the US standard is the other way round.

Also, in the UK, the full stop separates the quotation marks, whilst in the US, the full stop comes before both.

E.g. *'I told him "never come back here".'* in the UK or *"I told him 'never come back here.'"* in the US.

ii) Punctuation After Dialogue

If your dialogue is followed by a dialogue tag (*said, asked, replied* etc.), the dialogue finishes with a comma and the dialogue tag starts in the lower case, e.g. *'Look over there,' she said*. If the dialogue needs an exclamation or question mark, the narrative still begins with the lower case, e.g. *'Look over there!' she said*.

If the narrative following your dialogue describes an action other than speaking, the dialogue should end with a full stop (or a question mark or exclamation mark as appropriate), e.g. *'Fantastic!' He grinned*.

If the narrative includes both a dialogue tag and an action, the dialogue should end with a comma, e.g. *'Fantastic,' he said with a grin*.

iii) Punctuation Before Dialogue

When your dialogue tag introduces the speech, the dialogue always starts with a capital letter, and it is now common practice to use a comma as opposed to a colon, e.g. *He said, 'When are you coming over?'*

iv) Punctuation Within Dialogue

Keep your punctuation within your dialogue simple – commas and full stops. If neither a comma or full stop works, then use an en dash (–) with spaces either side if writing in the UK, or an em dash (—) with no spaces if writing in the US. People do not tend to speak with semicolons, and so they should not appear in written dialogue. However, a colon can be used if necessary, such as when introducing a list.

When your character is addressing another character by name, use a comma beforehand to make this clear. For example, consider the difference between *'I know Chris.'* and *'I know, Chris.'* The first is a discussion between two people about Chris, the second is addressing Chris.

Note the comma or full stop at the end of the dialogue goes before the quotation mark.

v) Text Between Dialogue

Occasionally, dialogue is broken up by an action. If the action occurs between sentences, the punctuation is straightforward, e.g. *'I'm really glad we did this.' He leaned forward and kissed her. 'I've had a great time.'*

However, if the action interrupts a sentence, commas and lower case are used, e.g. *'Go home,' she said, 'to your wife.'*

vi) Punctuation Of Phrases Quoted Within Text Or Dialogue

The main point here is to separate which part of the sentence the punctuation refers to. Therefore, punctuation which is part of a quote, such as an exclamation or question mark, is placed within the quotation marks, and punctuation which relates to the surrounding text is placed outside the quotation marks:

'She says there'll be tools to help me find "a better work/life balance"!'

vii) Contractions

Contractions in dialogue help to make your characters' words flow more naturally, e g. *isn't, didn't, haven't* etc. and it is now standard to use contractions unless you wish to emphasize something by spelling the words out in full. Consider:

'I haven't forgotten anything.' versus *'I have not forgotten anything.'*

The first is a character reassuring someone, while the second is defensive.

6. Possessive Apostrophes

Apostrophes are used to indicate possession, but care needs to be taken not to confuse a possessive with a plural. Plurals do not contain an apostrophe unless it's a possessive plural.

In the case of a possessive plural, be careful to ensure the apostrophe is in the right place. I often see *her parent's house* which suggests the house belongs to only one of her parents instead of both: *her parents' house*.

When using the possessive form of a noun that already ends with an *s*, consider how you would say the word when speaking aloud, e.g. *Russ's house* as opposed to *The Perkins' house*. Of course, this may change depending on your character's accent (or characters' accents), the key is to go with which sounds most natural to you as the author.

A note on *its*: only use an apostrophe if *it's* is the contracted form of it is. Even though *its* is often a possessive, there is no apostrophe, e.g. *its screen is too small*.

7. En Dashes And Em Dashes

An en dash is longer than a hyphen and shorter than an em dash – and is based on the width of the letter *n*. An em dash is longer — the width of the letter *m*.

In UK English, en dashes are used as parenthetical dashes – instead of brackets – including a space before and after. But take care to ensure the parenthetical clause is enclosed both at the start and the end by an en dash; they often start with an en dash and end with a comma which creates confusion. In US English, em dashes are used (without spaces).

An en dash is also used in the UK to add an extra bit of information at the end of a sentence or in place of a semicolon, especially in contemporary fiction. The US publishing industry uses an em dash.

Em dashes are used in both versions of English when dialogue or action is suddenly broken off or interrupted, e.g. *'I'm sorry about that first night, I didn't understand—'*

To find the en dash on your computer, go to the *Insert* tab in Word, select *Symbol*, then *More Symbols*. It can be found under *Font: (normal text) Subset: General Punctuation*.

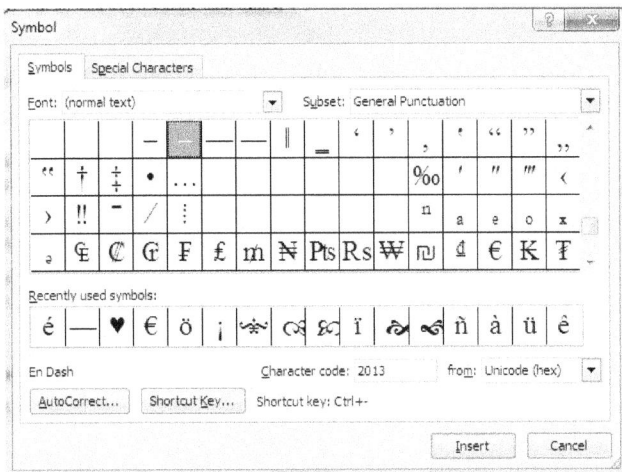

I use it often when I'm writing or editing and have found it easier to assign a shortcut to save time. To do this, go to the *File* tab, select *Options* then *Customize Ribbon*, which will open the following dialogue box:

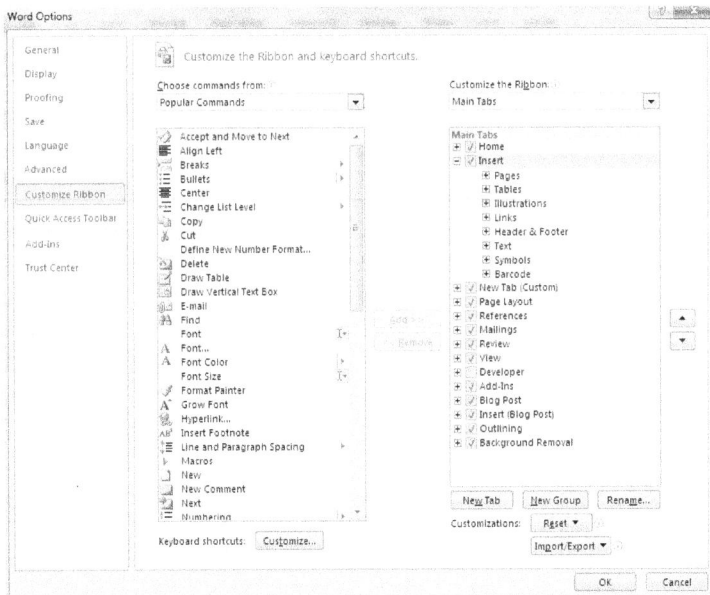

Choose *Keyboard Shortcuts: Customize* at the bottom towards the left, which gives you the following screen:

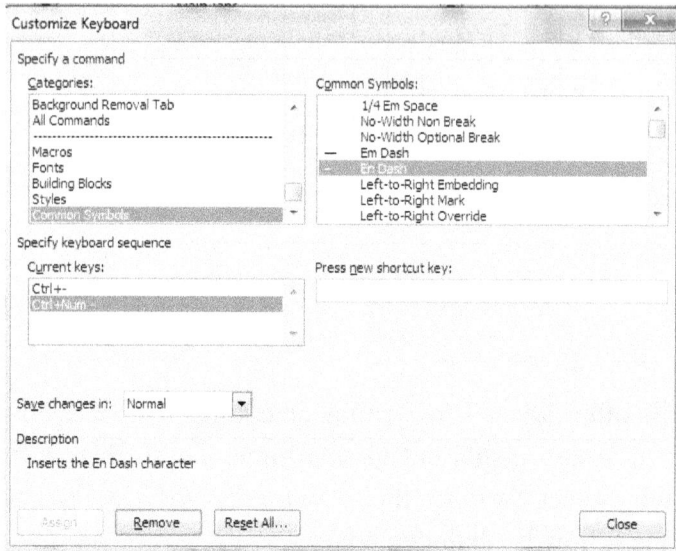

Scroll down in the *Categories:* box to *Common Symbols* and highlight it (it's at the very end), then select *En Dash* in the box on the right. This will then bring up any shortcuts already set (usually *Ctrl* and *Num*). As you can see here, I have also added *Ctrl* and - as my shortcut. To set a shortcut don't type it out, but go to the *Press new shortcut key* box and press the appropriate keys together.

While you are here, you can also set a shortcut for em dashes by selecting it in the *Common Symbols* box and adding your shortcut as above. For this one I use *Ctrl* and =

8. Ellipses

An ellipsis (a series of dots . . .) is used when dialogue tails off or the action pauses, but be careful not to overuse – many readers (and publishers) do not like them.

The correct format for an ellipsis is to use spaces before and between the three dots, as well as a space afterwards if the narrative or dialogue continues . . .

There is no space at the end when it forms the end of a paragraph or is closed by quotation marks, nor is there a further full stop, comma or exclamation mark, although occasionally a question mark can be used. Using this format with spaces gives the best look to a paperback book, allowing the justification of the text to be well balanced. It is especially important for e-readers as you cannot dictate where a line will end. If you don't put a space before the ellipsis, it can look like a full stop, followed by a couple of dots on the next line. Leaving out the spaces between the dots connects two words and pushes the line out of balance.

If you have used any other format than the one above in your manuscript, the easiest way to replace them is to select the ellipsis in your text, copy it (*ctrl* and *c*), paste (*ctrl* and *v*) into the *Find What* box, then enter " . . . " without the quotation marks (space dot space dot space dot space) in the *Replace With* box and click *Replace All*. For some reason, just putting the dots in the *Find What* box, even in exactly the same format you have used in your manuscript, does not always work.

Find and Replace		
Find	Replace	Go To
Find what:	...	
Replace with:	...	
More >>	Replace Replace All Find Next Cancel	

The next stage is to format those instances where quotation marks directly follow the ellipsis. The step you have just carried out above puts in an extra space before the closing quotation mark. Enter the new format of ellipsis followed by a quotation mark (. . . " or . . . ' as appropriate) into the *Find What* box, then repeat it in the *Replace With* box, omitting the space between the last dot and the closing quotation mark. If you have both dialogue and quotations within your text then do this for both options.

Find and Replace		
Find	Replace	Go To
Find what:	...'	
Replace with:	...'	
More >>	Replace Replace All Find Next Cancel	

Then do the same for ellipses at the beginning of dialogue (' . . . in the *Find* box and ' . . . in the *Replace* box).

4. Gremlins

1. Started To/Began To

2. Repetition

3. Overused Words

4. Which Or That?

5. While Or Whilst?

6. Among Or Amongst?

7. Affect Or Effect?

8. Round Or Around?

9. Me Or I?

10. May Or Might?

11. Lie Or Lay?

12. Couple Was Or Couple Were?

13. A Or An?

1. Started To/Began To

If one of your characters starts or begins to do something, it infers they do not finish. Do they really start something, or do they actually do it? Delete all instances of started/began unless your character truly only begins the action.

2. Repetition

Do you have a favourite word or phrase? Does it appear over and over again? Do you have the same adjective in two consecutive sentences? Do you have a number of paragraphs starting with *I, he* or *she*? If so, this quickly becomes boring for your reader, and the instances of these words will jump out at them, distracting them from your story. It can be hard to spot them yourself, and this is where an editor or trusted beta reader is invaluable.

3. Overused Words

Some very common words are just (like this one!) impossible to avoid writing, and most need to come out when you are editing:

even, just, now, only, really, very, that.

If you're not sure if you need it or not, take it out. If the text does need it, it will be obvious on your next read through and you can put it back. To be really strict you could do a *Find and Replace*; putting each of the offending words in the *Find* box in turn (remembering to leave a space on either side of the word to avoid affecting words such as seven, justice etc.) and leaving the *Replace* box empty. Then you'll *know* you've got them all.

Also, *that* is overused and can often be omitted or replaced with *which*, especially in UK English (see next section).

Further words to reduce are *could*, *look* and *smile*. Is there another word that would work? In the case of *look*, maybe *glance* would be better, or *stare*, *gaze*, *peer* etc. Try to mix up your language, although without making it contrived.

4. Which Or That?

In defining clauses (clauses which can't be left out without affecting the sentence's meaning) either *which* or *that* can be used. It is good practice when writing in UK English to choose *which* wherever possible, although sometimes only *that* will do. In US English, *that* is the preferred option.

E.g. *There is a local service which would be more suitable* versus *There is a local service that would be more suitable.*

In non-defining clauses (clauses which add detail to the sentence without affecting the meaning if they are omitted) *which* is always used, whether writing in UK or US English.

E.g. *I was at the bottom edge of Hanging Wood, which covered the valley side, and it was steep.*

5. While Or Whilst?

Strictly speaking, *while* is used for action taking place during a time, whereas *whilst* is used for action taking place during an action, but in UK English *while* can be used for both.

6. Among Or Amongst?

Among is the earlier word, and the most common. *Amongst* is more modern and is not used as often, (and is not used in US English at all) but there is no difference between their meanings and the choice between them is purely down to personal preference as to which flows better in your text.

7. Affect Or Effect?

These are often confused, which is unfortunate as their meanings are very different. *Affect* is usually a verb meaning *make a difference to*, whereas *effect* is used as both a noun and verb to indicate a result of an action.

8. Round Or Around?

In UK English, *round* and *around* have two different meanings. *Round* is used for definite, specific movement (e.g. I turned round), whereas *around* is a more general term (e.g. I wandered around for an hour or so).

However, in US English, the two words are handled differently, and *around* is the usual form in most contexts. *Round* is more informal and is only used in specific expressions, such as *all year round* and *going round in circles*.

9. Me Or I?

Most people are comfortable with using *I* as the subject in a sentence and *me* as the object, but what about when there are two objects?

For example, *'Yes, darling, come and sit with Dad and—'* Should it be *Dad and I* or *Dad and me*? The easiest way of working out if *me* or *I* is correct, is to repeat the sentence without the *Dad and* and see which word fits. Therefore, *'Yes, darling, come and sit with me'* leads to *'Yes, darling, come and sit with Dad and me.'*

10. May Or Might?

Strictly speaking, *may* is the present tense and *might* past tense. However, these days they are virtually interchangeable and either can be used unless you have strong feelings either way.

There is more of a difference between *may have* and *might have*. If the details of a situation are not known at the time of writing or speaking, either can be used, e.g. *By the time he comes home, he may have worked out what he wants* can also be written *By the time he comes home, he might have worked out what he wants.*

If the event or situation did *not* happen, then use *might have*, e.g. *If England had scored that penalty we might have won the World Cup.*

11. Lie Or Lay?

In the present tense, lie refers to the subject of a sentence, whereas lay needs an object, but confusingly, lay is also the past form of lie. Therefore, your character will lie down (or lay down in the past) but will lay a plate on the table in the present (although laid it in the past).

12. Couple Was Or Couple Were?

This depends on the rest of the sentence and whether the couple is/are being treated as a single entity or two people. The same principle applies to crews, teams, crowds etc.

E.g. *The crew was getting restless* when they are treated as one, or *as the crew took their turns to clap him on the back* when treated as a number of individuals.

13. A Or An?

Traditionally, *an* was always used when the following word began with a vowel or an *h*, but this can interrupt the flow of narrative in a novel. When writing fiction consider how you would say the phrase aloud. If you would say *a*, then write *a*, e.g. *"I've booked us into a hotel."* If you would say *an*, then write *an*, e.g. *"I use an older version of Word."*

Formatting

Once you are sure your editing is complete, the next stage is to format your book for paperback (the Amazon company CreateSpace is the most popular choice for indie authors as there are no set-up costs. Readers can order their book from any Amazon site and it will be printed and sent direct to them), Kindle (the largest market for most indie authors) and EPUB. The most common site for EPUB books is Smashwords, which will convert your Word file and distribute to a large number of online bookstores, including Barnes & Noble (Nook), Kobo and iBooks.

The LionheART Guide to Formatting by Karen Perkins has been written as a companion guide to this editing guide and is a comprehensive, step-by-step guide to professionally formatting e-books and paperbacks.

To find out more about the full range of LionheART Publishing Guides, please visit:
www.karenperkinsauthor.com/lionheart

The LionheART
Guide to
Formatting

Karen Perkins

LionheART Publishing House

Covers

I cannot stress enough how important it is to get the cover for your book right. As independent authors, our biggest challenge is to find readers, and we find most of our readers online.

Your cover not only needs to look fantastic as a paperback, but also needs impact as a thumbnail. If someone is browsing through Amazon, iBooks, Barnes & Noble, Kobo or any of the other major online bookstores, they will not click on your book if the cover doesn't make them look twice. On top of that, a poor cover will mark your book as self-published, and many readers will then expect the writing, editing and formatting to be poor and pass your book by – often erroneously – but they'll never find that out unless they read the book.

Once the reader has bought or downloaded your book, your cover still needs to work for you – whether on your reader's bookshelf or on their e-reader (often in black and white). After all, as authors we want our books to be read – and hopefully reviewed, too!

Reviews

Thank you for buying and reading this editing guide. If you found it useful, please consider leaving a rating and review on the site where you bought it. All genuine comments and feedback are extremely important to Karen Perkins and are very welcome. Thank you.

About the Author

Karen Perkins is the international award-winning and bestselling author of six fiction titles in the Valkyrie Series of Caribbean pirate adventures and the Yorkshire Ghost Stories. All of her fiction has appeared at the top of bestseller lists on both sides of the Atlantic with over 200,000 downloads so far.

Her first Yorkshire Ghosts novel – *Thores-Cross* – is a silver medal winner for European Fiction in the 2015 Independent Publisher Book Awards, and *Dead Reckoning: A Caribbean Pirate Adventure* reached the top 50 in the UK Kindle chart as part of *The Hot Box* set that also included work by international bestselling thriller authors David Leadbeater, John Paul Davis and Steven Bannister.

See more about Karen Perkins, including contact details, on her websites:
www.lionheartgalleries.co.uk
www.karenperkinsauthor.com

Karen is on Social Media:

Facebook:
www.facebook.com/LionheartPublishing
www.facebook.com/Yorkshireghosts
www.facebook.com/ValkyrieSeries

Twitter:
@LionheartG

Books By Karen Perkins

Non-Fiction
The LionheART Guide To Editing Fiction, UK Edition
(Available as e-book and paperback)
The LionheART Guide To Editing Fiction, US Edition
(Available as e-book and paperback)

The LionheART Guide To Formatting
(Paperbacks, Epubs and Kindle) – Available in paperback

The LionheART Guide to Formatting Paperbacks
(Available as e-books)
The LionheART Guide to Formatting EPUBs
(Available as e-books)
The LionheART Guide to Formatting for Kindle
(Available as e-books)

**To find out more about the full range of LionheART
Publishing Guides, please visit:
www.karenperkinsauthor.com/lionheart**

Fiction

Yorkshire Ghost Stories – Available as e-books and paperback
Knight of Betrayal
Thores-Cross
Cursed (short story)

**To find out more about the full range of books in the Yorkshire Ghost Series, including upcoming titles, please visit:
www.karenperkinsauthor.com/yorkshire-ghosts**

Valkyrie Series
Look Sharpe!
Ill Wind
Dead Reckoning

The Valkyrie Series: The First Fleet (Look Sharpe!, Ill Wind & Dead Reckoning)

Where Away – a FREE Valkyrie short story (see below)

**To find out more about the full range of books in the Valkyrie Series, including upcoming titles, please visit:
www.karenperkinsauthor.com/valkyrie**

Where Away is being offered FREE for readers of the Valkyrie Series and will not be released separately—if you would like to read it, please order your copy from Karen's website:
www.karenperkinsauthor.com/valkyrie

Bibliography

There are many useful reference books and websites available to help us, this list details my favourite and most reliable sources of reference.

Magrs, Paul, and Bell, Julia. 2001. *The Creative Writing Coursebook.* London: Macmillan

Oxford University Press. 2005. *Fowler's Modern English Usage.* New York: Oxford University Press

Oxford University Press. 2004. *New Hart's Rules.* Oxford: Oxford University Press

Oxford University Press. 2005. *New Oxford Dictionary For Writers And Editors.* Oxford: Oxford University Press

Wiley Publishing, Inc 2007. *Copyediting & Proofreading For Dummies.* Indiana: Wiley Publishing, Inc

University of Chicago, The. 2010 *The Chicago Manual of Style 16th Edition.* Chicago: The University of Chicago Press

http://www.oxforddictionaries.com/

http://www.urbandictionary.com/

www.ingramcontent.com/pod-product-compliance
Lightning Source LLC
Chambersburg PA
CBHW060144050426
42448CB00010B/2286